# Everyday Coasters

Designs by Carole Rodgers

T4-ABM-941

**Size:** Coasters: 3¾ inches W x 3¾ inches H (9.5cm x 9.5cm)
Coaster Box: 4¼ inches W x 3 inches H x 1 inch D (10.8cm x 7.6cm x 2.5cm)

**Skill Level:** Intermediate

## Materials
- 1 sheet 7-count plastic canvas
- Needloft® plastic canvas yarn as listed in color key
- #16 tapestry needle

## Cutting & Stitching

**1** Cut plastic canvas according to graphs (this page and page 2).

**2** Stitch pieces following graphs, working Smyrna Cross Stitches following stitch diagram.

**3** Using fern throughout, Overcast coasters. For coaster box, Whipstitch front and back to sides, then Whipstitch front, back and sides to base. Overcast remaining edges.

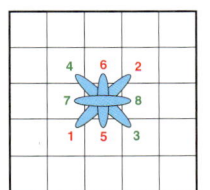

**Smyrna Cross Stitch**
Bring needle up at odd numbers and down at even numbers

**COLOR KEY**
| Yards | Plastic Canvas Yarn |
|---|---|
| 63 (57.7m) | ■ Fern #23 |

Color number given is for Needloft® plastic canvas yarn.

**Coaster Box Back**
27 holes x 19 holes
Cut 1

**Coaster**
25 holes x 25 holes
Cut 4

A Dozen Coaster Sets 1

**Coaster Box Front**
27 holes x 19 holes
Cut 1

**COLOR KEY**
| Yards | Plastic Canvas Yarn |
|---|---|
| 63 (57.7m) | ■ Fern #23 |

Color number given is for Needloft® plastic canvas yarn.

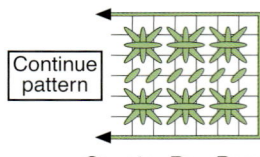

**Coaster Box Base**
27 holes x 6 holes
Cut 1

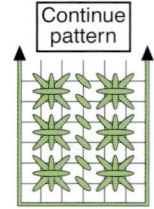

**Coaster Box Side**
6 holes x 19 holes
Cut 2

# Sunbonnet Susie
*Designs by Sandy Dye*

**Size:** **Coasters:** 3⅞ inches W x 3⅞ inches H (9.8cm x 9.8cm)
**Coaster Box:** 4¼ inches W x 2 inches H x 1⅛ inches D (10.8cm x 5.1cm x 2.9cm)
**Skill Level:** Beginner

## Materials
- 2½ sheets 7-count plastic canvas
- Needloft® plastic canvas yarn as listed in color key
- #16 tapestry needle

### Cutting & Stitching

**1** Cut plastic canvas according to graphs. Cut one 27-hole x 6-hole piece for holder base. Base will remain unstitched.

**2** Stitch coasters following graphs, working uncoded areas with baby blue Continental Stitches. Stitch one coaster as graphed. Stitch one coaster replacing watermelon with yellow and pink with lemon, one coaster replacing watermelon with royal and pink with bright blue, and one coaster replacing watermelon with bright purple and pink with lilac.

**3** When background stitching is completed, work black Backstitches for shoes and white Straight Stitches for dress accents.

**4** Using baby blue throughout, Overcast coasters. For coaster holder, Whipstitch front and back to sides, then Whipstitch front, back and sides to unstitched base. Overcast top edges.

2  A Dozen Coaster Sets

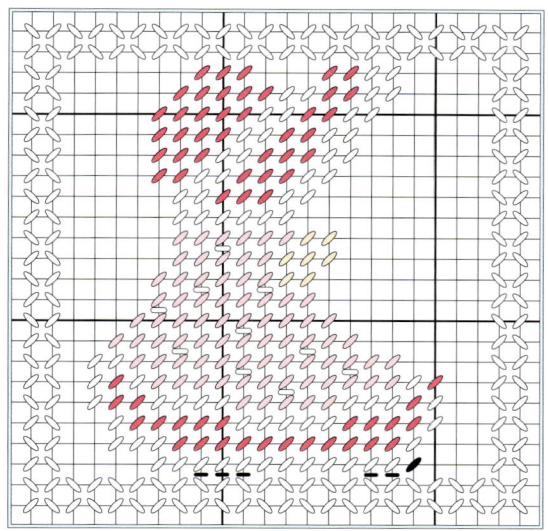

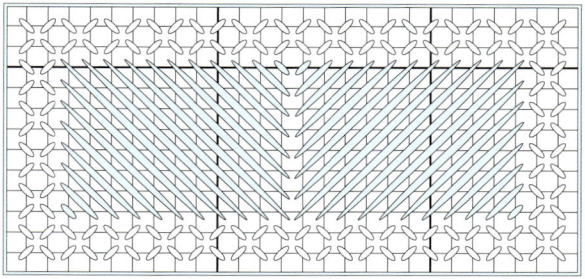

**Holder Front & Back**
27 holes x 13 holes
Cut 2

**Coaster**
25 holes x 25 holes
Cut 4
Stitch 1 as graphed
Stitch 1 replacing watermelon with
yellow and pink with lemon
Stitch 1 replacing watermelon with
royal and pink with bright blue
Stitch 1 replacing watermelon with
bright purple and pink with lilac

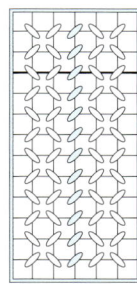

**Holder Side**
6 holes x 13 holes
Cut 2

| COLOR KEY | |
|---|---|
| **Yards** | **Plastic Canvas Yarn** |
| 1 (1m) | ■ Black #00 |
| 2 (1.9m) | ☐ Pink #07 |
| 2 (1.9m) | Lemon #20 |
| 2 (1.9m) | Royal blue #32 |
| 25 (22.9m) | ☐ Baby blue #36 |
| 21 (19.3m) | ☐ White #41 |
| 2 (1.9m) | Lilac #45 |
| 2 (1.9m) | ■ Watermelon #55 |
| 1 (1m) | ☐ Fleshtone #56 |
| 2 (1.9m) | Yellow #57 |
| 2 (1.9m) | Bright blue #60 |
| 2 (1.9m) | Bright purple #64 |
| | Uncoded areas are baby blue #36 Continental Stitches |
| ╱ | Black #00 Backstitch |
| ╱ | White #41 Straight Stitch |

Color numbers given are for Needloft® plastic canvas yarn.

A Dozen Coaster Sets **3**

# Roosters in a Nest

Designs by Ronda Bryce

**Size:** Coasters: 5⅛ inches W x 3⅞ inches H (13cm x 9.8cm), excluding rickrack
Nest: 1⅝ inches H x 4½ inches in diameter (4.1cm x 11.4cm)
**Skill Level:** Intermediate

## Materials

- 1 sheet 7-count plastic canvas
- 4-inch plastic canvas radial circle
- Needloft® plastic canvas yarn as listed in color key
- #16 tapestry needle
- 4 (⅝-inch/16mm) round black buttons with short shanks
- 12 inches (30.4cm) red jumbo rickrack
- Hand-sewing needle
- Black, red and green sewing thread

## Cutting & Stitching

**1** Cut plastic canvas according to graphs. Do not cut or stitch radial circle, which will be nest base.

**2** Following graphs throughout, stitch and Overcast rooster coasters and leaves, working Continental Stitches in uncoded areas as follows: coaster A with brown, coaster B with fern, coaster D with eggshell. Stitch nest side.

**3** Whipstitch side edges of nest side together, then Whipstitch bottom edge to unstitched base; Overcast top edge.

**4** For eyes, use hand-sewing needle and black thread to sew buttons in place where indicated on graphs.

**5** Cut rickrack in four 3-inch (7.6cm) lengths. Using hand-sewing needle and red thread, stitch to back sides of heads from arrow to arrow, turning ends under.

**6** Using hand-sewing needle and green thread, tack leaves to nest side opposite seam (see photo).

**7** Place rooster coasters in nest.

**Nest Leaf**
5 holes x 7 holes
Cut 6

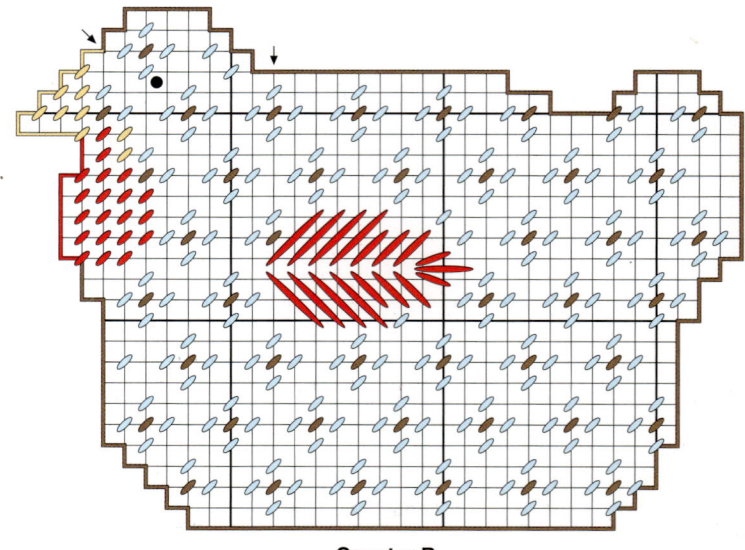

**Coaster B**
34 holes x 25 holes
Cut 1

4 A Dozen Coaster Sets

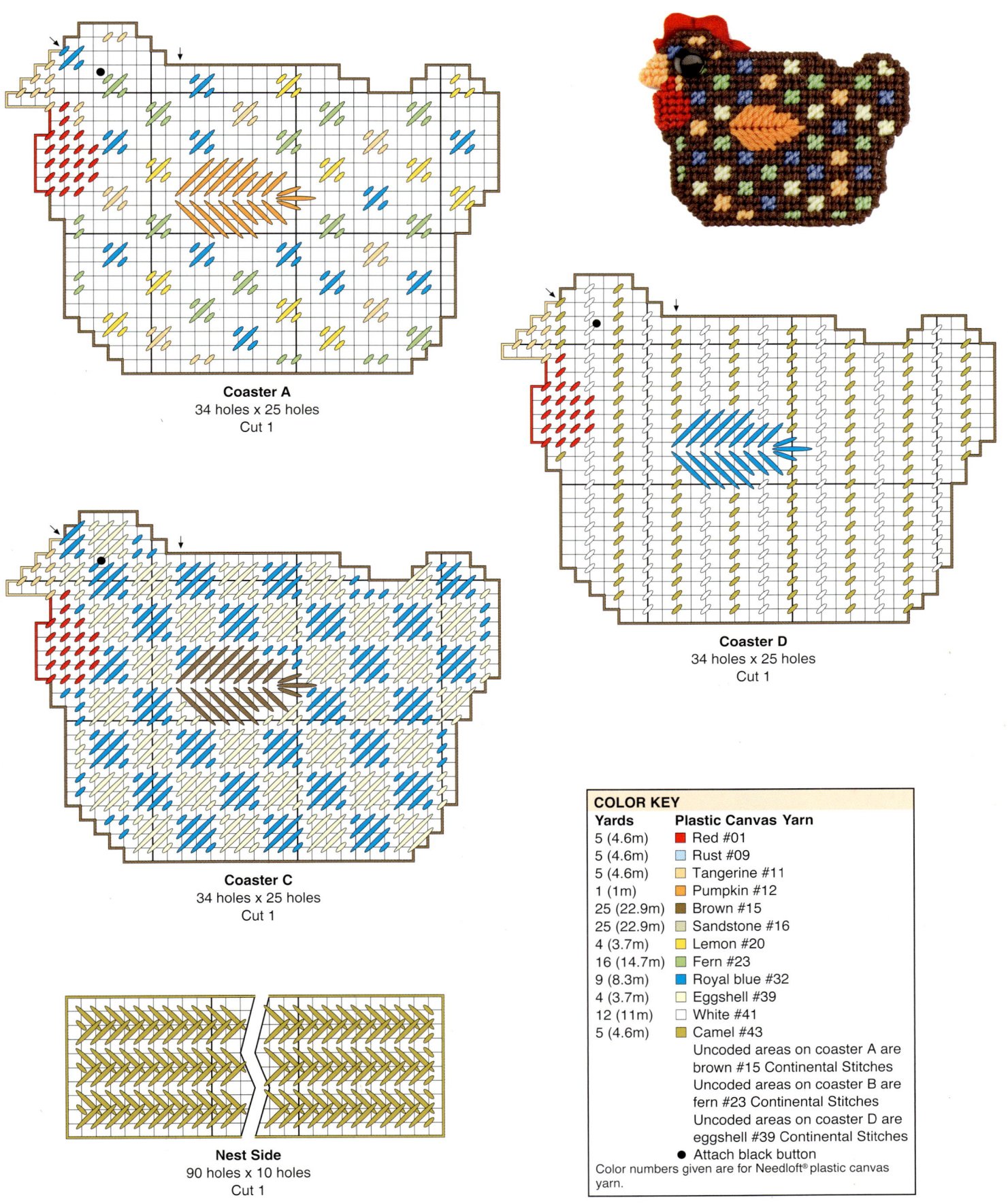

# Card Coasters

Designs by Nancy Barrett

**Size:** **Card Coasters:** 3⅜ inches W x 5⅛ inches H (8.6cm x 13cm)
**Holder:** 3⅞ inches W x 5½ inches H x 2 inches D (9.8cm x 14cm x 5.1cm)
**Skill Level:** Intermediate

## Materials
- 2 sheets 7-count plastic canvas
- Medium weight yarn as listed in color key
- #16 tapestry needle

### Cutting & Stitching

**1** Cut plastic canvas according to graphs, cutting out hole on holder front and back.

**2** Stitch holder pieces and card backs following graphs.

**3** Work uncoded areas on card fronts with white Continental Stitches. Stitch one card front as graphed. Stitch one card front replacing diamond with heart following heart motif graph. Stitch remaining two front pieces, replacing red with black and diamond with one each of spade and club motifs following graphs.

**4** For holder, using blue throughout, Overcast holes on holder front and back. With wrong sides facing, Whipstitch front and back to sides, then Whipstitch front, back and sides to base. Overcast top edges.

**5** For each card, Whipstitch wrong sides of one front and one back together with white.

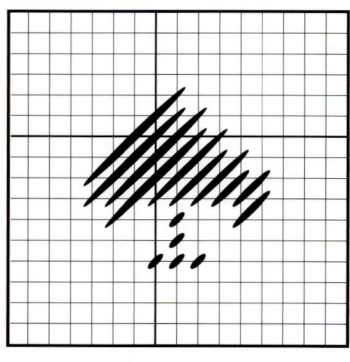
Spade Motif

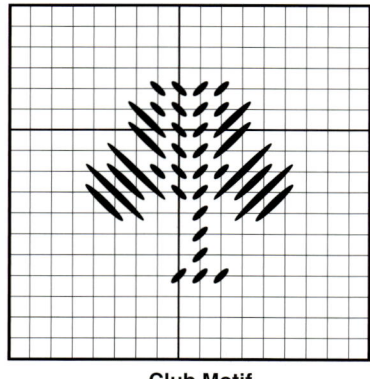
Club Motif

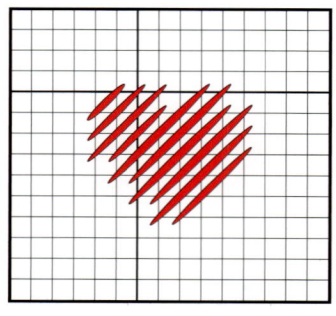
Heart Motif

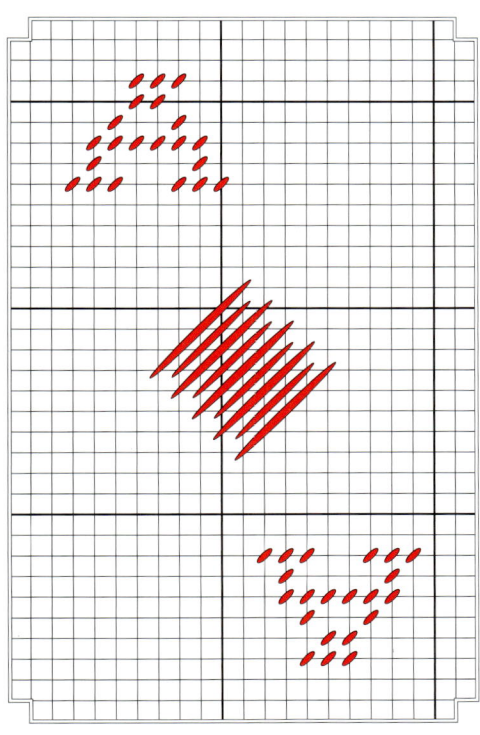

**Card Front**
22 holes x 34 holes
Cut 4
Stitch 1 as graphed
Stitch 1 replacing diamond motif
with heart motif
Stitch remaining 2 replacing red with black
and diamond with one each
of spade and club motifs

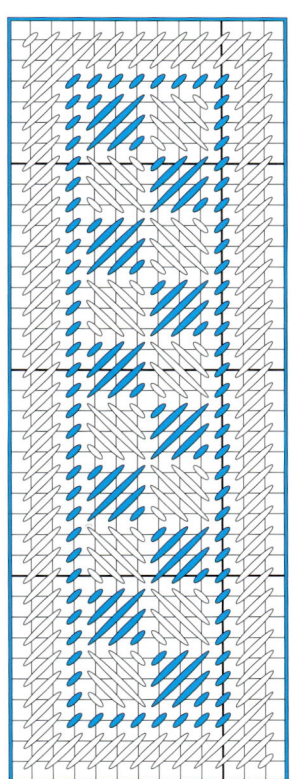

**Holder Side**
13 holes x 37 holes
Cut 2

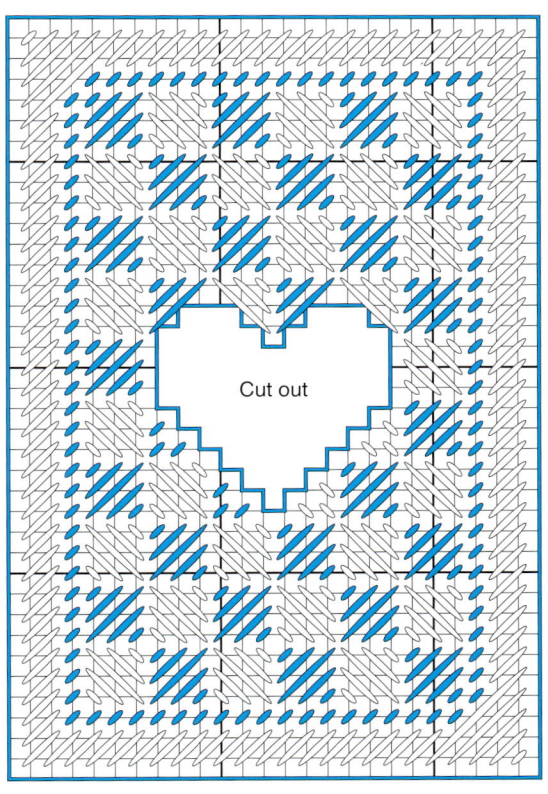

**Holder Front & Back**
25 holes x 37 holes
Cut 2

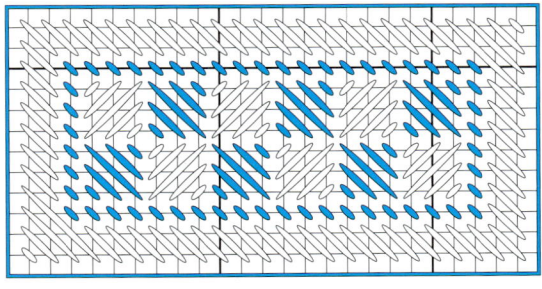

**Holder Base**
25 holes x 13 holes
Cut 1

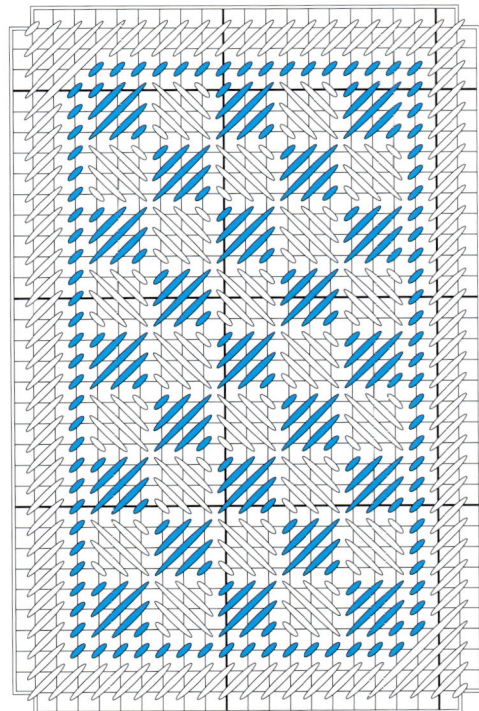

**Card Back**
22 holes x 34 holes
Cut 4

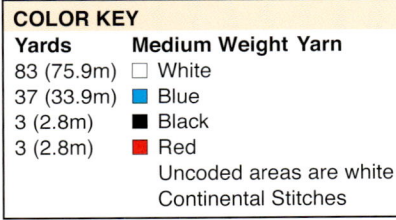

**COLOR KEY**
| Yards | Medium Weight Yarn |
|---|---|
| 83 (75.9m) | □ White |
| 37 (33.9m) | ■ Blue |
| 3 (2.8m) | ■ Black |
| 3 (2.8m) | ■ Red |

Uncoded areas are white
Continental Stitches

A Dozen Coaster Sets **7**

# The Cat's Meow

Designs by Kathy Wirth

**Size:** **Coasters:** 4 7/8 inches W x 4 3/8 H inches (12.4cm x 11.1cm)
**Holder:** 5 1/4 inches W x 3 7/8 inches H x 3 inches D (13.3cm x 9.8cm x 7.6cm)
**Skill Level:** Beginner

## Materials

- 3 sheets 7-count plastic canvas
- Needloft® plastic canvas yarn as listed in color key
- 6-strand embroidery floss as listed in color key
- #16 tapestry needle
- #20 tapestry needle
- 1½ (9 x 12-inch/22.9 x 27.9cm) sheets self-adhesive felt

## Cutting & Stitching

**1** Cut plastic canvas according to graphs. Cut one 20-hole x 19-hole piece for holder base. Base will remain unstitched.

**2** Stitch remaining pieces following graphs, working Continental Stitches in uncoded areas as follows: coasters with gray and holder pieces with bright blue.

**3** When background stitching is completed, use black yarn to embroider French Knots for fishes' eyes on holder front and back, and work Straight Stitches for pupils of eyes on coasters. Work Straight Stitches and Backstitches for mouth and whiskers on coasters with 6 strands black embroidery floss.

**4** Holding unstitched pieces behind stitched pieces, working through all thicknesses and using white throughout, Whipstitch long edges of unstitched base to straight bottom edges of front and back. Whipstitch short edges of sides to base; Whipstitch sides to front and back, easing as necessary to fit. Whipstitch/Overcast remaining edges of holder with white.

**5** Trace outline of coaster six times on paper side of self-adhesive felt; cut out inside traced lines. Holding one unstitched coaster behind each stitched coaster, Whipstitch through both thicknesses with adjacent colors.

**6** Remove paper backing from felt; adhere to backs of coasters.

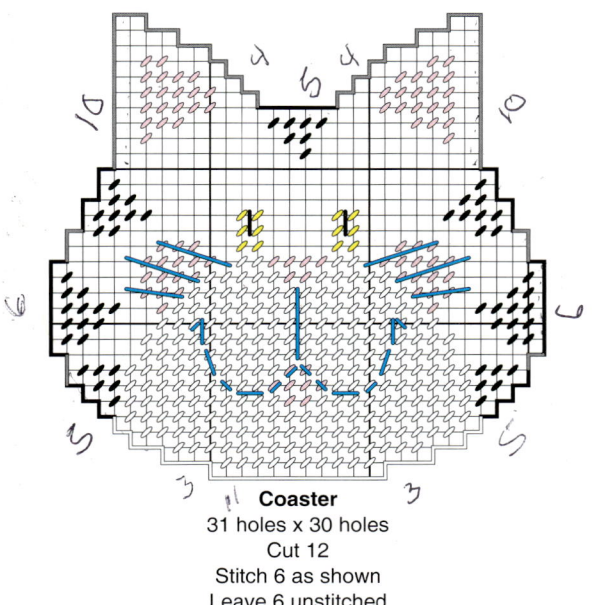

**Coaster**
31 holes x 30 holes
Cut 12
Stitch 6 as shown
Leave 6 unstitched

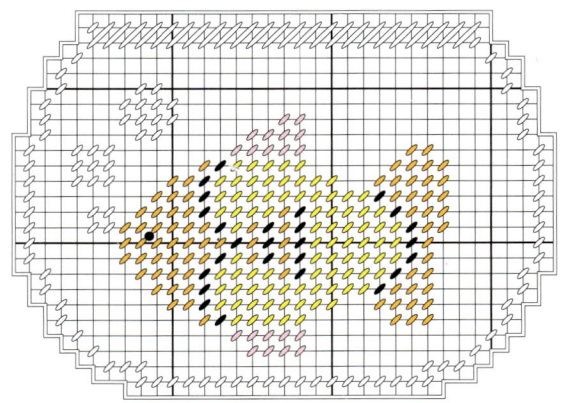

**Holder Front & Back**
34 holes x 25 holes
Cut 4
Stitch 2 as shown
Leave 2 unstitched

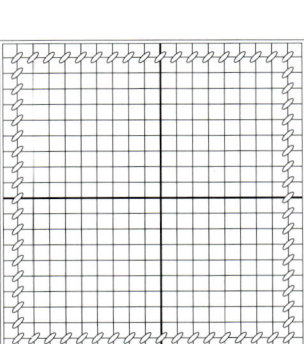

**Cat Coaster Set Holder Side**
19 holes x 20 holes
Cut 2

| COLOR KEY | |
|---|---|
| **Yards** | **Plastic Canvas Yarn** |
| 13 (11.9m) | ■ Black #00 |
| 9 (8.3m) | ▨ Pink #07 |
| 4 (3.7m) | ▨ Lemon #20 |
| 38 (34.8m) | ☐ White #41 |
| 3 (2.8m) | ▨ Bright orange #58 |
| 30 (27.5m) | Uncoded areas on coasters are gray #38 Continental Stitches |
| 19 (17.4m) | Uncoded areas on holder pieces are bright blue #60 Continental Stitches |
| | ╱ Black #00 Straight Stitch |
| | ╱ Gray #38 Whipstitch |
| | ● Black #00 French Knot |
| | **6-Strand Embroidery Floss** |
| 3 (2.8m) | ╱ Black Backstitch and Straight Stitch |
| Color numbers given are for Needloft® plastic canvas yarn. | |

**A Dozen Coaster Sets 9**

# Noah's Ark

**Designs by Carole Rodgers**

**Size:** **Elephant Coaster:** 4⅛ inches W x 3½ inches H (10.5cm x 8.9cm)
**Giraffe Coaster:** 3¾ inches W x 6 inches H (9.5cm x 15.2cm)
**Lion Coaster:** 3⅞ inches W x 3⅞ inches H (9.8cm x 9.8cm)
**Zebra Coaster:** 4¼ inches W x 4¼ inches H (10.8cm x 10.8cm)
**Coaster Holder:** 6¼ inches W x 5 inches H x 1¼ inches D (15.9cm x 12.7cm x 3.2cm)

**Skill Level:** Beginner

### Materials
- 2 sheets 7-count plastic canvas
- Needloft® plastic canvas yarn as listed in color key
- #16 tapestry needle
- Fabric glue

### Cutting & Stitching

**1** Cut pieces following graphs, carefully cutting out gray area on giraffe. Cut one 25-hole x 7-hole piece for coaster holder base. Base will remain unstitched.

**2** Work pieces following graphs. Overcast edges of coasters, dove and Noah with adjacent colors.

**3** Using adjacent colors and following assembly diagram, Whipstitch coaster holder pieces together. Overcast remaining edges.

**4** Glue dove and Noah to front of holder as shown in photo.

| COLOR KEY | |
|---|---|
| **Yards** | **Plastic Canvas Yarn** |
| 8 (7.4m) | ☐ Black #00 |
| 2 (1.9m) | ☐ Red #01 |
| 30 (27.5m) | ☐ Maple #13 |
| 5 (4.6m) | ☐ Brown #15 |
| 8 (7.4m) | ☐ Lemon #20 |
| 14 (12.9m) | ☐ Christmas green #28 |
| 10 (9.2m) | ☐ Silver #37 |
| 6 (5.5m) | ☐ Beige #40 |
| 12 (11m) | ☐ White #41 |
| 1 (1m) | ☐ Lilac #45 |
| 6 (5.5m) | ☐ Purple #46 |
| 1 (1m) | ☐ Fleshtone #56 |
| 2 (1.9m) | ☐ Bright blue #60 |
| | ╱ Black #00 Backstitch and Straight Stitch |
| 1 (1m) | Tangerine #11 Overcast |
| | ╱ Brown #15 Backstitch |
| | ● Black French Knot |
| Color numbers given are for Needloft® plastic canvas yarn. | |

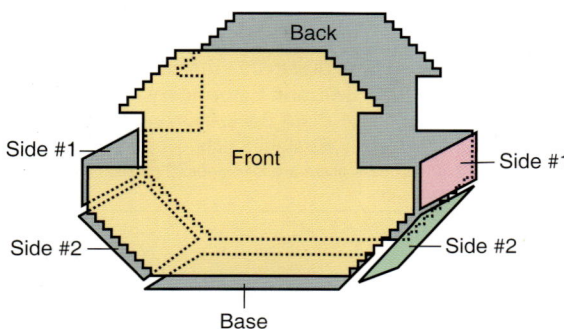

**Coaster Holder Assembly Diagram**
Pieces are shown in different colors for contrast; gray denotes wrong side

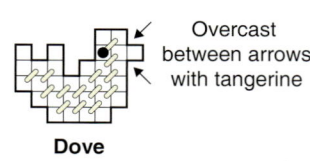

**Dove**
8 holes x 6 holes
Cut 1

Overcast between arrows with tangerine

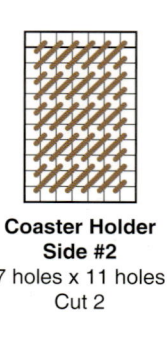

**Coaster Holder Side #2**
7 holes x 11 holes
Cut 2

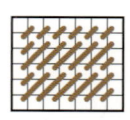

**Coaster Holder Side #1**
7 holes x 6 holes
Cut 2

# Eggs in a Basket

Designs by Vicki Blizzard

**Size:** **Coasters:** 3⅞ inches W x 4⅛ inches H (9.8cm x 10.5cm)
**Basket Holder:** 4⅜ inches W x 3 inches H x 1⅛ inches D (11.1cm x 7.6cm x 2.9cm)
**Skill Level:** Intermediate

## Materials
- 1½ sheets 7-count plastic canvas
- Medium weight yarn as listed in color key
- 9 x 12-inch (22.9 x 27.9cm) sheet white felt
- #16 tapestry needle
- Hot-glue gun

## Cutting & Stitching

**1** Cut and stitch plastic canvas according to graphs. Cut one 16-hole x 10-hole piece for holder base. Base will remain unstitched.

**2** Using white throughout, Whipstitch short edges of sides to short edges of unstitched base. Whipstitch front and back to sides and base, easing along side edges as necessary to fit; Overcast top edges.

**3** Overcast eggs with white and hearts with pink.

## Assembly

**1** Glue felt to backs of eggs; let dry. Trim edges to fit.

**2** Using photo as a guide, glue one heart each to holder front and back.

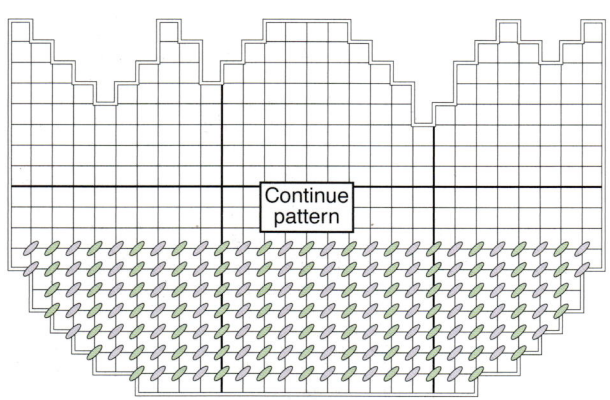

**Holder Front & Back**
28 holes x 18 holes
Cut 2

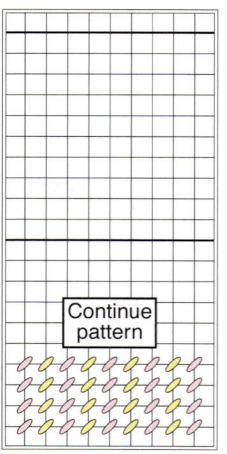

**Holder Side**
10 holes x 21 holes
Cut 2

12 A Dozen Coaster Sets

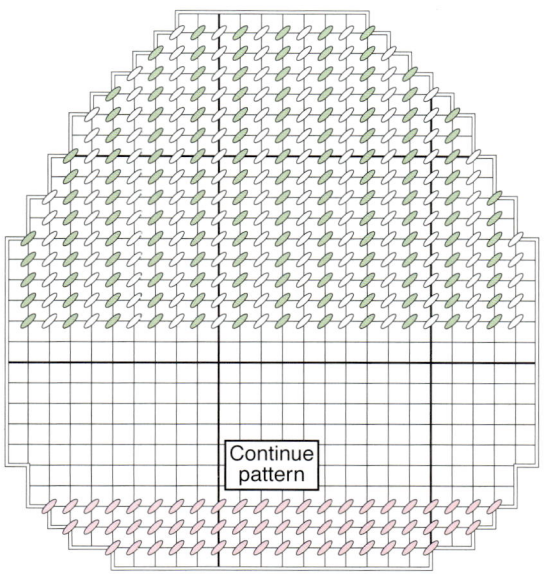

**Coaster A**
25 holes x 27 holes
Cut 1

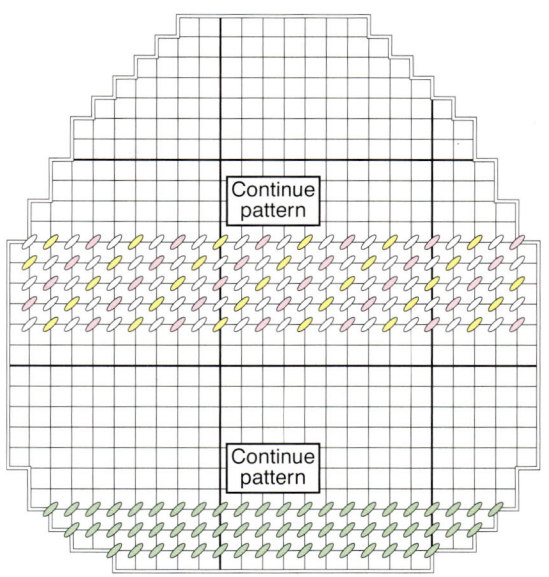

**Coaster B**
25 holes x 27 holes
Cut 1

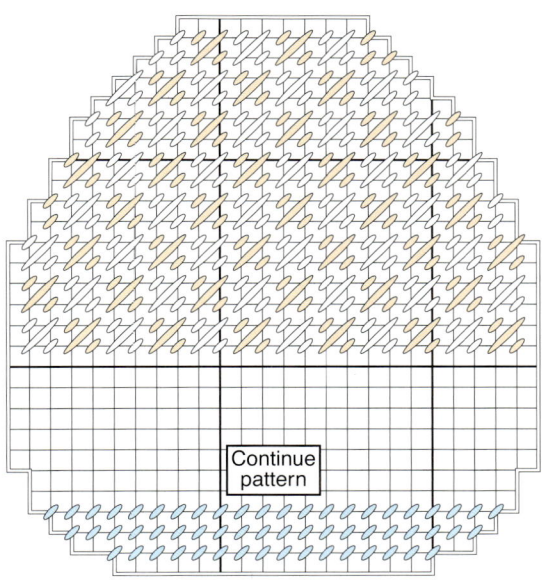

**Coaster C**
25 holes x 27 holes
Cut 1

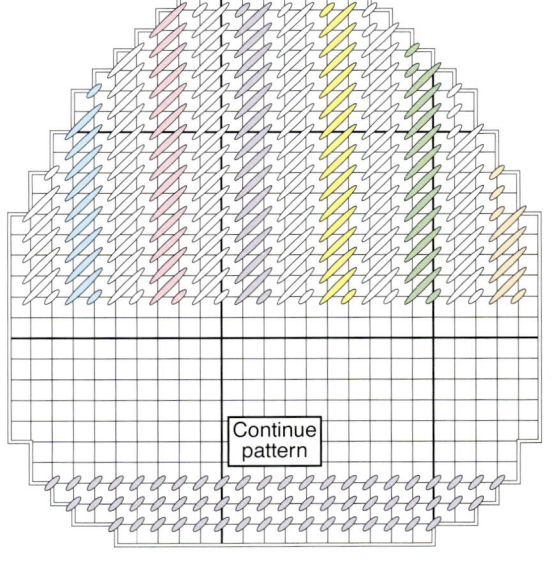

**Coaster D**
25 holes x 27 holes
Cut 1

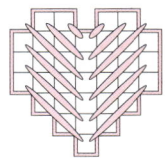

**Heart**
7 holes x 7 holes
Cut 2

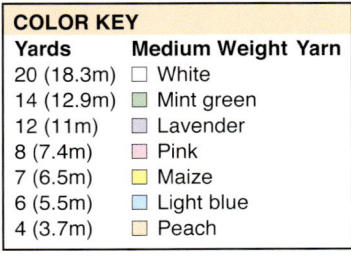

| COLOR KEY | |
|---|---|
| Yards | Medium Weight Yarn |
| 20 (18.3m) | ☐ White |
| 14 (12.9m) | ☐ Mint green |
| 12 (11m) | ☐ Lavender |
| 8 (7.4m) | ☐ Pink |
| 7 (6.5m) | ☐ Maize |
| 6 (5.5m) | ☐ Light blue |
| 4 (3.7m) | ☐ Peach |

A Dozen Coaster Sets 13

# Fruit Set

Designs by Michele Wilcox

**Size:** Coasters: 4 inches W x 4¾ inches H (10.2cm x 12.1cm)
Coaster Holder: 4¼ inches W x 2⅜ inches H x 1 inch D (10.8cm x 6cm x 2.5cm)
**Skill Level:** Beginner

## Materials
- 2 sheets 7-count plastic canvas
- Needloft® plastic canvas yarn as listed in color key
- #16 tapestry needle

## Cutting & Stitching

**1** Cut plastic canvas according to graphs. Cut one 28-hole x 6-hole piece for holder base. Base will remain unstitched.

**2** Stitch remaining pieces following graphs. When background stitching is completed, work black French Knots for watermelon seeds.

**3** Using fern throughout, Overcast coasters. For coaster holder, Whipstitch front and back to sides, then Whipstitch front, back and sides to base. Overcast top edges.

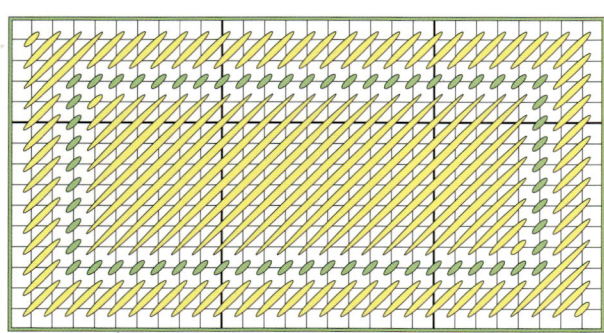

**Coaster Holder Front & Back**
28 holes x 15 holes
Cut 2

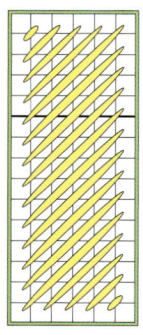

**Coaster Holder Side**
6 holes x 15 holes
Cut 2

**COLOR KEY**

| Yards | Plastic Canvas Yarn |
|---|---|
| 4 (3.7m) | ■ Red #01 |
| 2 (1.9m) | ■ Christmas red #02 |
| 1 (1m) | ■ Cinnamon #14 |
| 8 (7.4m) | ■ Gold #17 |
| 40 (36.6m) | ■ Lemon #20 |
| 6 (5.5m) | ■ Fern #23 |
| 1 (1m) | □ White #41 |
| 2 (1.9m) | ■ Watermelon #55 |
|  | Uncoded areas are lemon #20 Continental Stitches |
| 1 (1m) | ● Black #00 French Knot |

Color numbers given are for Needloft® plastic canvas yarn.

14 A Dozen Coaster Sets

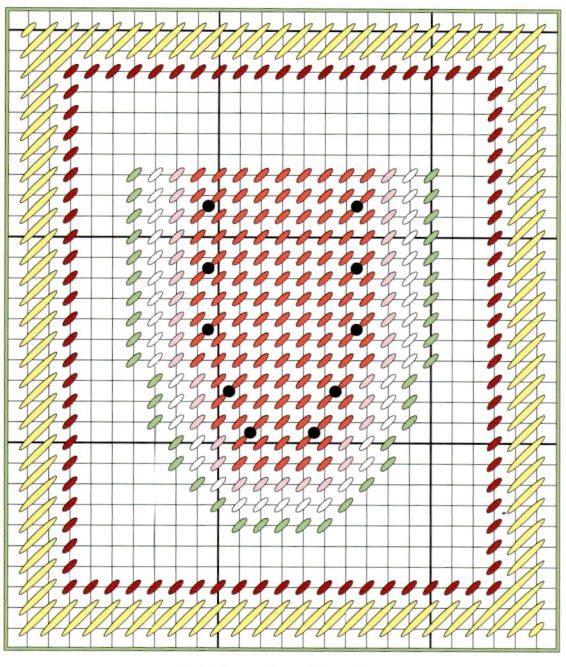

**Watermelon Coaster**
26 holes x 31 holes
Cut 1

**Apple Coaster**
26 holes x 31 holes
Cut 1

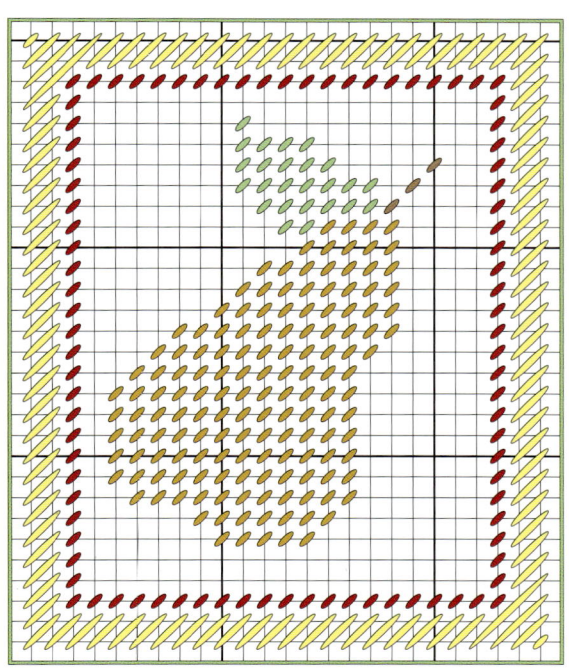

**Pear Coaster**
26 holes x 31 holes
Cut 1

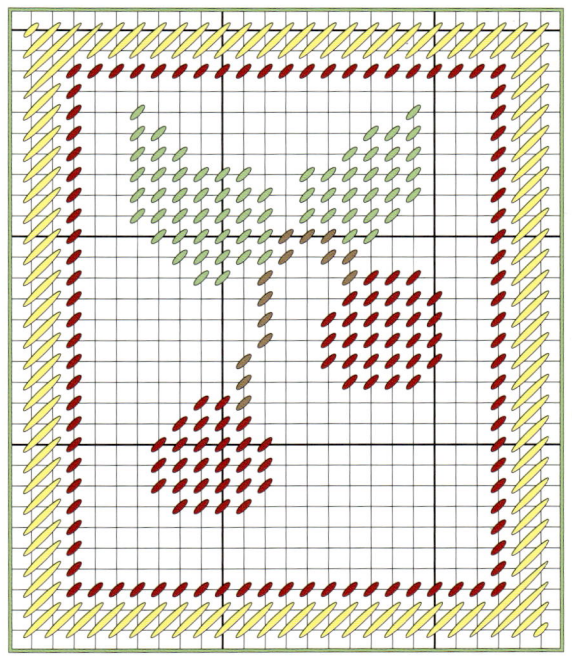

**Cherries Coaster**
26 holes x 31 holes
Cut 1

A Dozen Coaster Sets **15**

# In the Doghouse!

Designs by Deborah Scheblein

**Size:** **Coasters:** 4¼ inches W x 3¾ inches H (10.8cm x 9.5cm)
**Doghouse Holder:** 6 inches W x 5¾ inches H x 2¼ inches D (15.2cm x 14.6cm x 5.7cm)
**Skill Level:** Beginner

### Materials
- 1½ sheets 7-count plastic canvas
- Medium weight yarn as listed in color key
- #16 tapestry needle
- 2 (6mm) round black cabochons
- 7mm black pompom
- Brown felt
- Hot-glue gun

### Instructions

**1** Cut plastic canvas according to graphs (pages 17 and 18). Cut brown felt to fit coasters.

**2** Stitch and Overcast coasters following graphs, working uncoded areas with white Continental Stitches. Glue felt to back of each coaster.

**3** Stitch doghouse front, back, sides and base following graphs, working uncoded areas on front with brown Continental Stitches.

**4** Using red, Whipstitch front and back to sides, then Whipstitch front, back and sides to base. Overcast roof edges with brown and top edges of sides and back with red.

**5** Stitch and Overcast sign, bowl, grass, and dog front, back and muzzle following graphs, working uncoded background on sign with ecru Continental Stitches.

**6** When background stitching is completed, work brown Backstitches for letters on sign.

**7** Using photo as a guide, center and glue dog front to dog back, making sure bottom edges are even. Glue muzzle to dog front where indicated on graph with blue lines.

**8** Glue cabochons to head for eyes and pompom to muzzle for nose where indicated on graphs.

**9** Using photo as a guide, glue dog and bowl to doghouse front, making sure bottom edges are even. Glue sign over door. Center and glue grass to back, making sure bottom edges are even.

16 A Dozen Coaster Sets

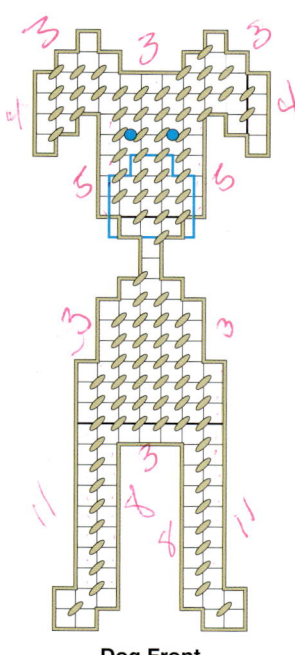

**Dog Front**
11 holes x 29 holes
Cut 1

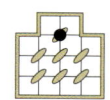

**Dog Muzzle**
4 holes x 4 holes
Cut 1

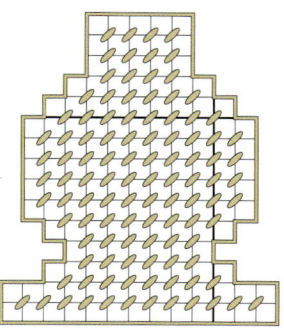

**Dog Back**
13 holes x 15 holes
Cut 1

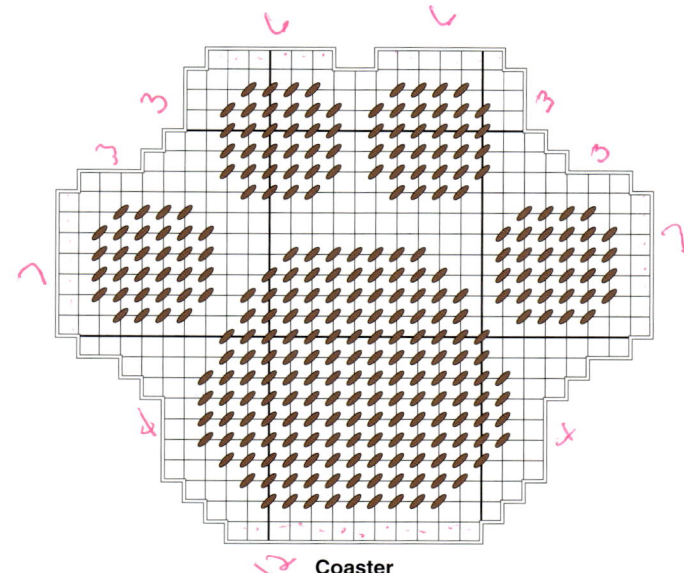

**Coaster**
28 holes x 24 holes
Cut 4

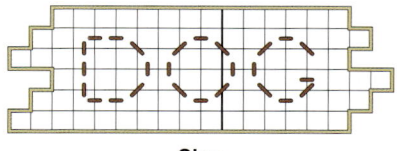

**Sign**
18 holes x 6 holes
Cut 1

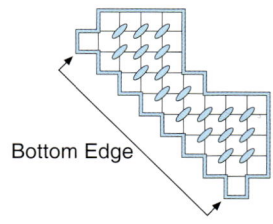

**Dog Bowl**
9 holes x 9 holes
Cut 1

| COLOR KEY | |
|---|---|
| **Yards** | **Medium Weight Yarn** |
| 26 (23.8m) | ■ Brown |
| 24 (22m) | ■ Red |
| 7 (6.5m) | ■ Tan |
| 3 (2.8m) | ■ Green |
| 1 (1m) | ■ Medium blue |
| 16 (14.7m) | Uncoded areas on coasters are white Continental Stitches |
| 2 (1.9m) | Uncoded background on sign is ecru Continental Stitches |
| | Uncoded areas on doghouse front are brown Continental Stitches |
| | ╱ Brown Backstitch |
| | ╱ White Overcast |
| | ● Attach black cabochon |
| | ● Attach black pompom |

A Dozen Coaster Sets 17

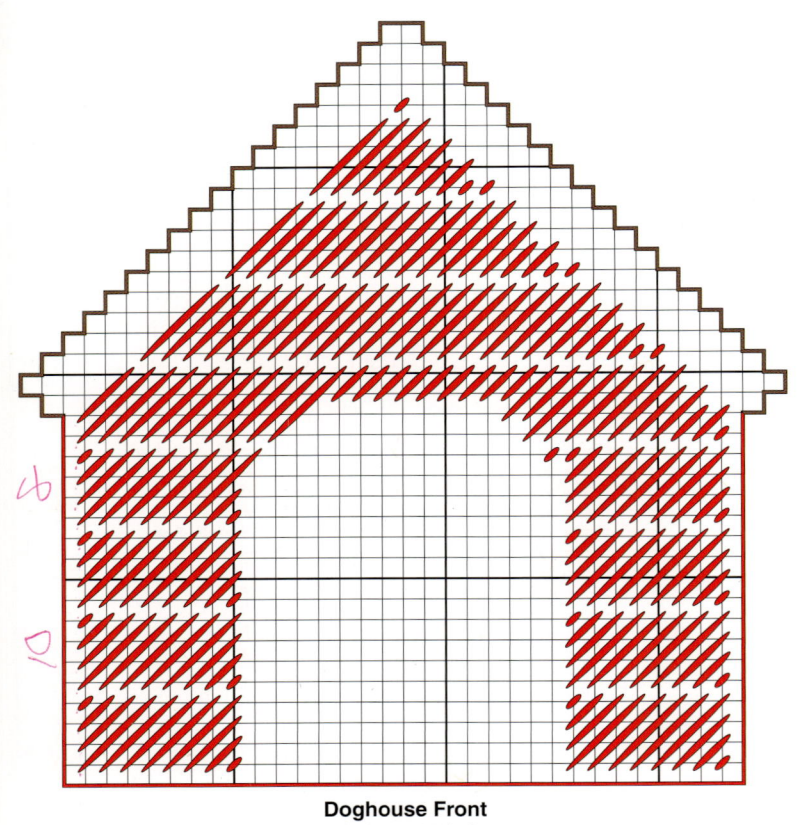

**Doghouse Front**
36 holes x 37 holes
Cut 1

| COLOR KEY | |
|---|---|
| **Yards** | **Medium Weight Yarn** |
| 26 (23.8m) | ■ Brown |
| 24 (22m) | ■ Red |
| 7 (6.5m) | ■ Tan |
| 3 (2.8m) | ■ Green |
| 1 (1m) | ☐ Medium blue |
| 16 (14.7m) | Uncoded areas on coasters are white Continental Stitches |
| 2 (1.9m) | Uncoded background on sign is ecru Continental Stitches |
| | Uncoded areas on doghouse front are brown Continental Stitches |
| ╱ | Brown Backstitch |
| ╱ | White Overcast |
| ● | Attach black cabochon |
| ● | Attach black pompom |

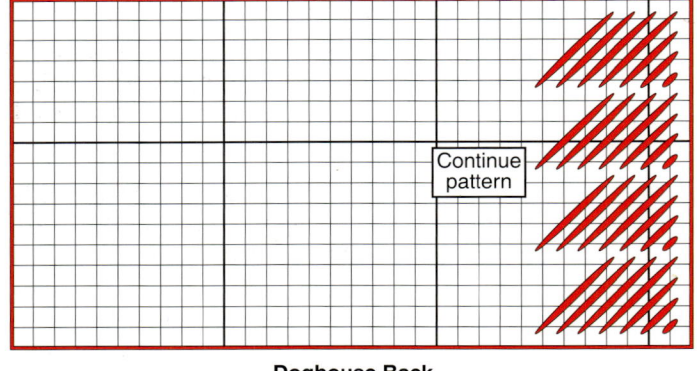

**Doghouse Back**
32 holes x 17 holes
Cut 1

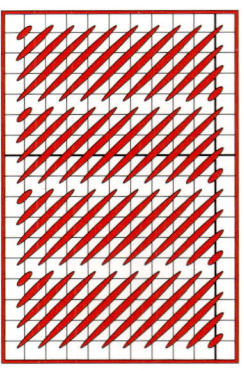

**Doghouse Side**
11 holes x 17 holes
Cut 2

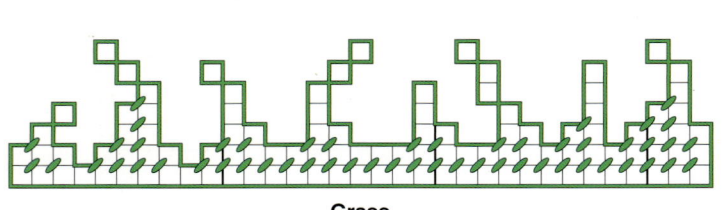

**Grass**
33 holes x 7 holes
Cut 1

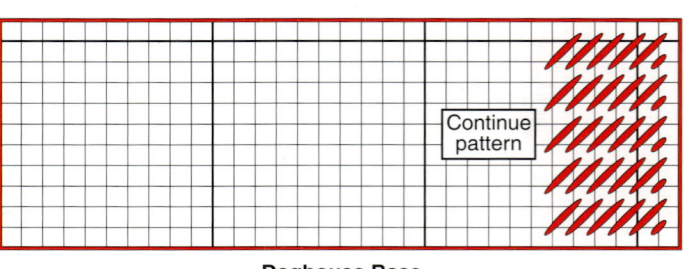

**Doghouse Base**
32 holes x 11 holes
Cut 1

18 A Dozen Coaster Sets

# Pumpkin Pleasers

Designs by Phyllis Dobbs

### Size:
**Coasters:** 4¼ inches W x 3⅞ inches H
**Coaster Holder:** 5⅛ inches W x 2⅛ inches H x 2⅛ inches D (13cm x 5.4cm x 5.4cm)
**Napkin Holder:** 7 inches W x 5 inches H x 2 inches D (17.8cm x 12.7cm x 5.1cm)
### Skill Level: Beginner

## Materials
- 2 sheets 7-count plastic canvas
- Needloft® plastic canvas yarn as listed in color key
- #16 tapestry needle

## Cutting

**A:** For napkin holder front and back, cut two according to graph (page 20).
**B:** For napkin holder sides, cut two pieces 9 holes x 12 holes (no graph).
**C:** For napkin holder base, cut one piece 12 holes x 45 holes (no graph).
**D:** For coasters, cut four according to graph (page 20).
**E:** For coaster holder front and back, cut two according to graph (page 20).
**F:** For coaster holder sides, cut two according to graph (page 20).
**G:** For coaster holder base, cut one piece 13 holes x 33 holes (no graph).

## Stitching

**1** C and G pieces will remain unstitched. Stitch B pieces with Christmas green Continental Stitches. Stitch remaining pieces following graphs. Overcast D pieces.

**2** Using photo and assembly diagram as a guide, Whipstitch corresponding pieces together with adjacent colors; Overcast unfinished edges.

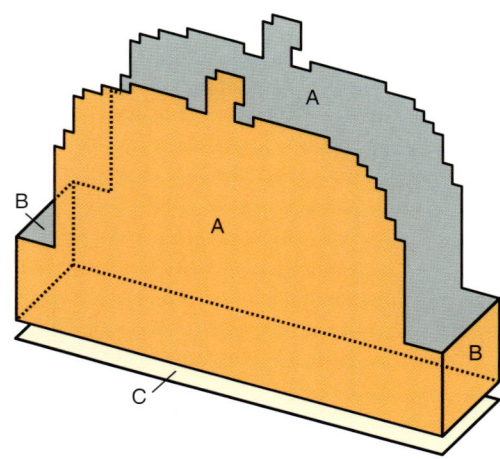

**Napkin Holder Assembly Diagram**

A Dozen Coaster Sets 19

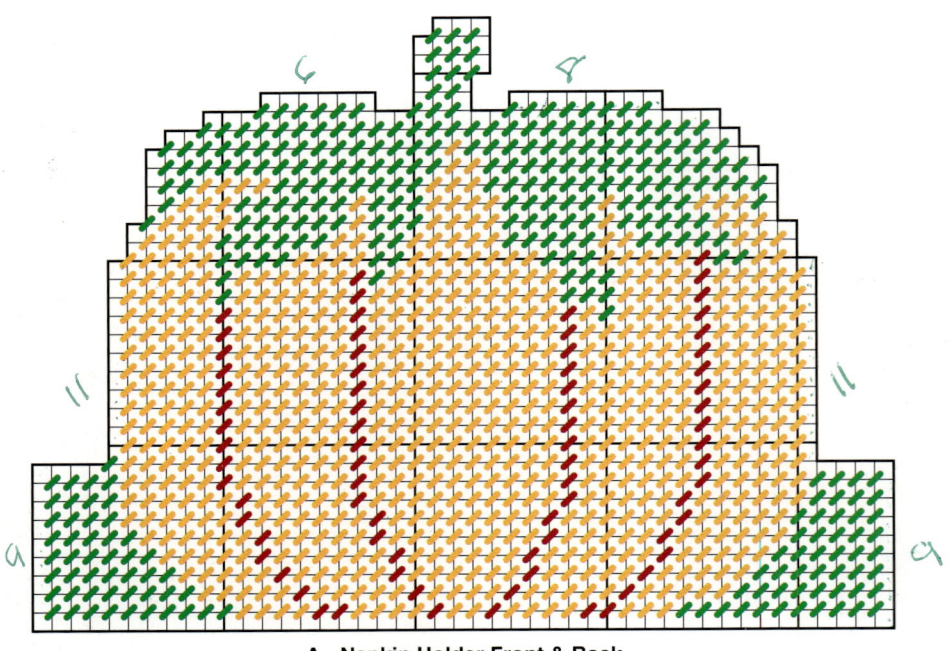

**A - Napkin Holder Front & Back**
45 holes x 33 holes
Cut 2

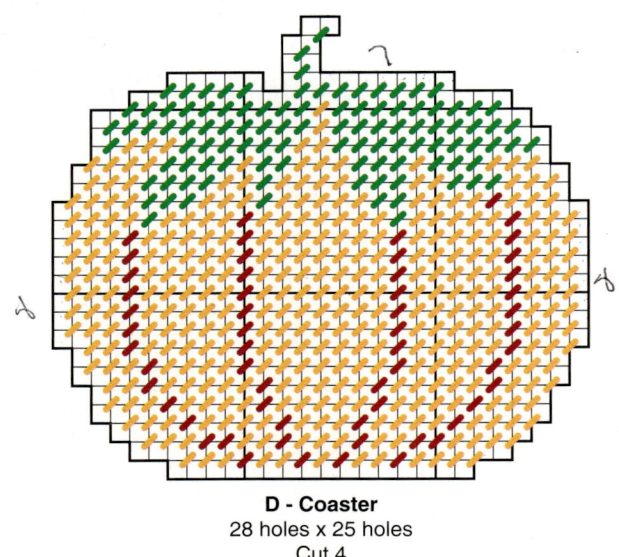

**D - Coaster**
28 holes x 25 holes
Cut 4

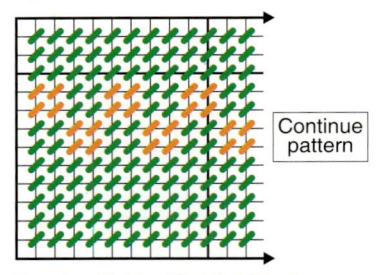

**E - Coaster Holder Front & Back**
33 holes x 13 holes
Cut 2

**F - Coaster Holder Side**
13 holes x 13 holes
Cut 2

| COLOR KEY | |
|---|---|
| **Yards** | **Plastic Canvas Yarn** |
| 64 (58.5m) | ▨ Tangerine #11 |
| 42 (38.4m) | ▨ Christmas green #28 |
| 10 (9.2m) | ▨ Bittersweet #52 |

Color numbers given are for Needloft® plastic canvas yarn.

20 A Dozen Coaster Sets

# Roly-Poly Santa

Designs by Laura Oversby

**Size:** **Coasters:** 3¾ inches W x 4⅜ inches H (9.5cm x 11.1cm)
**Holder:** 4⅜ inches W x 1½ inches H x 1½ inches D (11.1cm x 3.8cm x 3.8cm)
**Skill Level:** Beginner

## Materials
- 1 sheet 7-count plastic canvas
- Medium weight yarn as listed in color key
- #16 tapestry needle
- 1 sheet white felt
- Hot-glue gun

## Instructions

**1** Cut four coasters and one front from plastic canvas according to graphs.

**2** Cut two 9-hole x 9-hole pieces for holder sides and two 28-hole x 9-hole pieces for holder back and base. Base will remain unstitched.

**3** Cut four pieces of felt slightly smaller than coasters.

**4** Stitch back and sides with white Continental Stitches. Stitch holder front and Santa coasters following graphs, working uncoded areas with red Continental Stitches.

**5** Overcast coasters. For holder, Whipstitch front and back to sides, then Whipstitch front, back and sides to unstitched base. Overcast top edges.

**6** Glue felt to backs of coasters.

| COLOR KEY |  |  |
|---|---|---|
| Yards | | Medium Weight Yarn |
| 20 (18.3m) | ■ | Red |
| 15 (13.8m) | □ | White |
| 2 (1.9m) | ■ | Black |
| 2 (1.9m) | ▨ | Light peach |
| 1 (1m) | ▨ | Light yellow |
| | | Uncoded areas are red Continental Stitches |

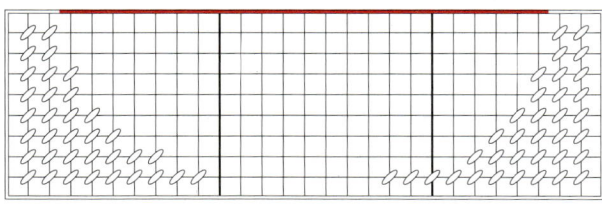

**Holder Front**
28 holes x 9 holes
Cut 1

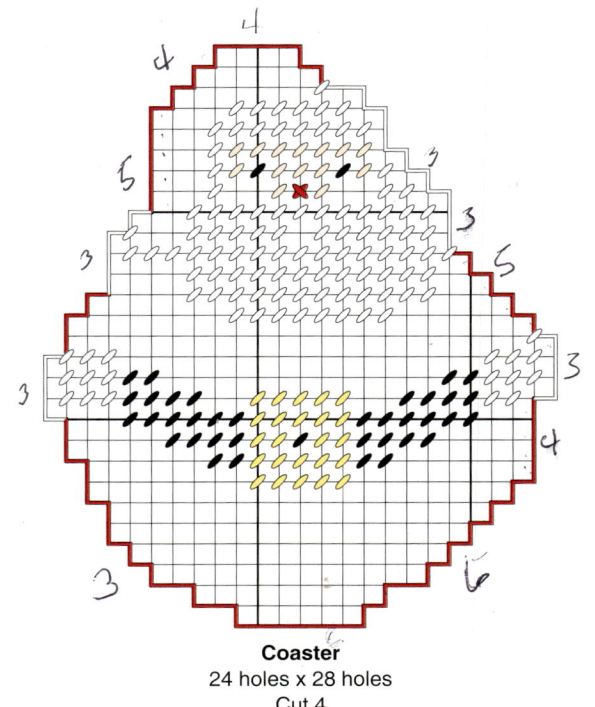

**Coaster**
24 holes x 28 holes
Cut 4

A Dozen Coaster Sets 21

# Maple Leaves

Designs by Linda Wyszynski

**Size:** Coasters: 4¼ inches W x 4 inches H
(10.8cm x 10.2cm)
Holder: 5¾ inches W x 4⅛ inches H x
1⅝ inches D (14.6cm x 10.5cm x 4.1cm)
**Skill Level:** Beginner

## Materials
- ❏ 2 sheets 7-count plastic canvas
- ❏ Medium weight yarn as listed in color key
- ❏ DMC #5 pearl cotton as listed in color key
- ❏ #16 tapestry needle
- ❏ 4-pound-test fishing line or invisible thread

## Cutting & Stitching

**1** Cut plastic canvas according to graphs. Cut one 30-hole x 9-hole piece for holder base.

**2** Holder base, six coasters (backing pieces), two holder sides, and one each of holder front and back (liner pieces) will remain unstitched.

**3** For holder, stitch one front, one back and two sides following graphs.

**4** Place unstitched holder backing pieces behind corresponding stitched pieces. Working through all thicknesses, Whipstitch front and back to sides, then Whipstitch front, back and sides to base. Whipstitch together top edges.

**5** Following graph, stitch one leaf with gold and one with blue-green yarn. Reverse four leaves; stitch two with purple, one with blue-green and one with burgundy. Stitch all stems with blue-green pearl cotton.

**6** Work pearl cotton Backstitches for leaf veins using graph as a guide, but stitching veins on each leaf differently.

**7** Matching edges, Whipstitch one unstitched leaf backing to each stitched leaf, working all edges with adjacent colors.

**8** Using photo as a guide, securely attach one purple leaf and one blue-green leaf to holder front with fishing line, making sure bottom edges of leaves are not below bottom edge of holder.

**9** Place maple leaf coasters in holder.

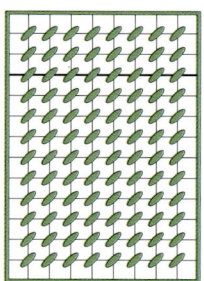

**Holder Side**
9 holes x 13 holes
Cut 4, stitch 2

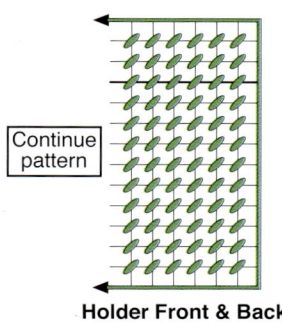

**Holder Front & Back**
30 holes x 13 holes
Cut 4, stitch 2

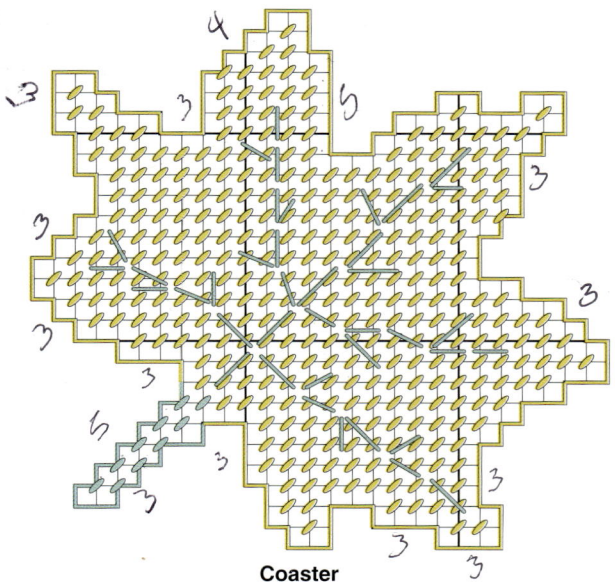

**Coaster**
27 holes x 26 holes
Cut 12, stitch 6
Stitch 1 with gold and
1 with blue-green
Reverse 4
Stitch 2 with purple
1 with burgundy
1 with blue-green

| COLOR KEY |  |
|---|---|
| **Yards** | **Medium Weight Yarn** |
| 35 (32m) | Blue-green |
| 22 (20.2m) | Gold |
| 22 (20.2m) | Purple |
| 22 (20.2m) | Burgundy |
|  | **#5 Pearl Cotton** |
| 28 (25.7m) | Blue-green #502 |
|  | Blue-green #502 Backstitch |

A Dozen Coaster Sets 23

## Getting Started

### Before You Cut

Buy one brand of canvas for each entire project as brands can differ slightly in the distance between bars. Count holes carefully from the graph before you cut, using the bolder lines that show every 10 holes. These 10-count lines begin from the left side for vertical lines and from the bottom for horizontal lines. Mark canvas before cutting; then remove all marks completely before stitching. If the piece is cut in a rectangular or square shape and is either not worked, or worked with only one color and one type of stitch, the graph may not be included in the pattern. Instead, the cutting and stitching instructions are given in the general instructions or with the individual project instructions.

### Covering the Canvas

Bring needle up from back of work, leaving a short length of yarn on back of canvas; work over short length to secure. To end a thread, weave needle and thread through the wrong side of your last few stitches; clip. Follow the numbers on the small graphs beside each stitch illustration; bring your needle up from the back of the work on odd numbers and down through the front of the work on even numbers. Work embroidery stitches last, after the canvas has been completely covered by the needlepoint stitches.

### Shopping for Supplies

For supplies, first shop your local craft and needlework stores. Some supplies may be found in fabric, hardware and discount stores. If you are unable to find the supplies you need, please visit AnniesCatalog.com.

## Basic Stitches

**Continental** 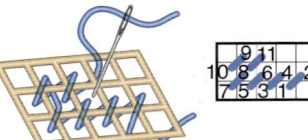 **Cross**

**Long** 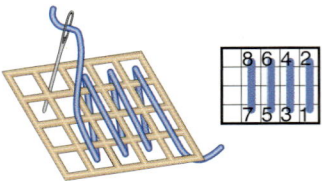 **Slanted Gobelin**

**Whipstitch**  **Overcast**

## Embroidery Stitches

**Backstitch** 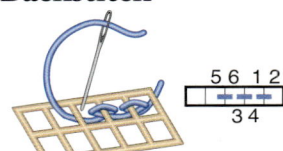 **Lazy Daisy**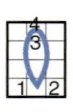

**Straight** 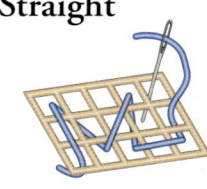 **French Knot**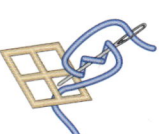

**METRIC KEY:**
millimeters = (mm)    meters = (m)
centimeters = (cm)    grams = (g)

---

**Annie's®** *A Dozen Coaster Sets* is published by Annie's, 306 East Parr Road, Berne, IN 46711. Printed in USA. Copyright © 2013, 2016 Annie's. All rights reserved. This publication may not be reproduced in part or in whole without written permission from the publisher.

**RETAIL STORES:** If you would like to carry this pattern book or any other Annie's publications, visit AnniesWSL.com

Every effort has been made to ensure that the instructions in this pattern book are complete and accurate. We cannot, however, take responsibility for human error, typographical mistakes or variations in individual work. Please visit AnniesCustomerCare.com to check for pattern updates.

ISBN: 978-1-59635-830-0